BETSY &
GIULIO MAESTRO

# The Story of the
# Statue of
# Liberty

LOTHROP, LEE & SHEPARD BOOKS
NEW YORK

For Marcello Maestro,
who inspired this book

**Acknowledgments**
Three reference books in particular were of great help in preparing the text and
illustrations for *The Story of the Statue of Liberty:*
*Statue of Liberty* by Oscar Handlin and the Editors of the Newsweek Book Division,
New York: Newsweek Book Division, 1971
*Statue of Liberty* by Charles Mercer
New York: G.P. Putnam's Sons, 1979
*In Search of Liberty, The Story of the Statue of Liberty and Ellis Island*
by James R. Bell and Richard I. Abrams
Garden City, New York: Doubleday & Company, Inc., 1984
   Besides providing detailed information about the Statue of Liberty, these books
contain photographs and drawings from the nineteenth century which were
invaluable in the preparation of the illustrations for this book. The works of a number
of photographers and artists of the period provide a unique record of the stages of
construction of the Statue of Liberty. These photographs and drawings may be found
in the collections of the Museum of the City of New York and in the Rare Book
Division of the New York Public Library.

Library of Congress Cataloging in Publication Data. Maestro, Betsy. The Statue of
Liberty. Summary: Describes the creation of the huge statue given by France to the
United States and its erection in New York Harbor as a symbol of liberty. 1. Statue
of Liberty (New York, N.Y.)—Juvenile literature. 2. Bartholdi, Frédéric Auguste,
1834–1904—Juvenile literature. 3. New York (N.Y.)—Buildings, structures, etc.—
Juvenile literature. [1. Statue of Liberty (New York, N.Y.) 2. National monuments.
3. Statues] I. Maestro, Giulio, ill. II. Title. NB553.B3A75  1986  730'.92'4  85-11324
ISBN 0-688-05773-X  ISBN 0-688-05774-8 (lib. bdg.)

# The Story of the Statue of Liberty

The Statue of Liberty stands on an island in New York
Harbor.   She is a beautiful sight to all who pass by her.
Each year, millions of visitors ride the ferry out to the island.
They climb to the top of the statue and enjoy the lovely view.

A young French sculptor named Frédéric Auguste Bartholdi visited America in 1871.   When he saw Bedloe's Island in New York Harbor, he knew it was just the right place for a statue he wanted to build.

Bartholdi had created many other statues and monuments, but this one was to be very special.   It was to be a present from the people of France to the people of America, as a remembrance of the old friendship between the two countries.

When Bartholdi got back to Paris, he made sketches and some small models. The statue would be a woman whom he would call Liberty. She would be a symbol of the freedom in the New World. She would hold a lamp in her raised hand to welcome people who came to America. She would be *Liberty Enlightening the World*.

15

The statue would be very large and very strong.   Bartholdi wanted people to be able to climb up inside the statue and look out over the harbor from the crown and torch.

Many well-known artists, engineers, and craftsmen gave him ideas about how to build the statue.   First, a huge skeleton was constructed from strong steel.

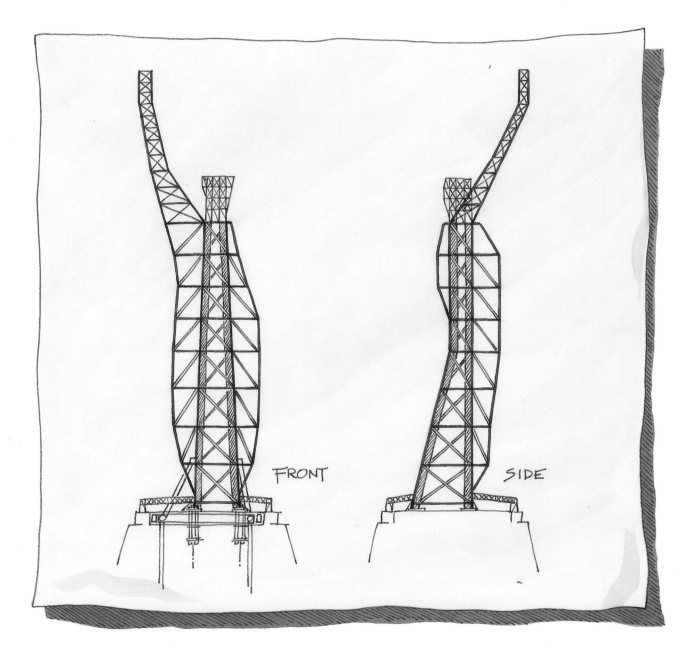

FRONT

SIDE

Many people worked together in a large workshop. Some worked on Liberty's head and crown. Others worked on her right hand which would hold the torch.

In her left hand she would hold a tablet with the date
July 4, 1776, written on it.   This is when the Declaration of
Independence was signed.

The arm holding the torch was sent to Philadelphia
for America's 100th birthday celebration in 1876.
Afterward, it stood in Madison Square in New York City
for a number of years.

Liberty's head was shown at the World's Fair in Paris
during this time. Visitors were able to climb inside and look
around. In this way, money was raised to pay for the statue.

Then, skin of gleaming copper was put onto the skeleton and held in place with iron straps. As the huge statue grew, all of Paris watched with great fascination.

Finally, in 1884, Liberty was completed. There was a big celebration in Paris. Many famous people came to see her. Only a few had the energy to climb all the way to the crown— 168 steps!

Then began the hard work of taking Liberty apart for the long voyage across the Atlantic Ocean. Each piece was marked and packed into a crate. There were 214 crates in all. They were carried by train and then put on a ship to America.

28

But in America people had lost interest in the Statue of Liberty. Money had run out and work on Bedloe's Island had stopped. The base for the statue was not finished.   With the help of a large New York newspaper, the money was raised.
People all over the country, including children, sent in whatever they could.   By the time the ship reached New York in 1885, it was greeted with new excitement.

The work on the island went on and soon the pedestal was completed. Piece by piece, the skeleton was raised. Then the copper skin was riveted in place. Liberty was put back together like a giant puzzle. The statue had been built not once, but twice!

At last, in 1886, Liberty was standing where she belonged.
A wonderful celebration was held.   Boats and ships filled
the harbor.   Speeches were read, songs were sung.
Bartholdi himself unveiled Liberty's face and she stood,
gleaming in all her glory, for everyone to see.
There was a great cheer from the crowd.
Then President Grover Cleveland gave a speech.

Over the years, immigrants have arrived to begin new lives
in America.   To them, the Statue of Liberty is a symbol of all
their hopes and dreams.   She has welcomed millions
of people arriving in New York by ship.

Every year, on the Fourth of July, the United States of America celebrates its independence.   Fireworks light up the sky above New York Harbor.   The Statue of Liberty is a truly unforgettable sight—a symbol of all that is America.

# ADDITIONAL INFORMATION
# ABOUT THE STATUE OF LIBERTY

## *Table of Dates*

□ □ □ □ □ □
• • •

**1834**
Frédéric Auguste Bartholdi is born on
August 2.

•

**1865**
Édouard de Laboulaye gives Bartholdi
idea for statue.

•

**1871**
Bartholdi makes first visit to America
and sees Bedloe's Island.

•

**1875**
Bartholdi completes first model.
Franco-American Union becomes
official sponsor of project. Work on
actual statue begins.

•

**1876**
Forearm and torch are displayed in
Philadelphia and then New York. On
July 4, Bartholdi visits Bedloe's Island
and decides how to position statue.

**1877**
American committee is formed to
sponsor construction of pedestal.
Bedloe's Island is named official site.

•

**1878**
Head of statue is exhibited in Paris.

•

**1880-1881**
Franco-American Union raises money
for statue. Lottery is held in France to
support statue.

•

**1883**
Ground-breaking takes place on
Bedloe's Island. Emma Lazarus writes
"The New Colossus" for the Pedestal
Fund.

•

**1884**
Statue is completed and officially
presented to the United States at Paris
Ceremony. Work on pedestal begins.

**1885**
Statue is dismantled for overseas voyage. The *New York World* helps to raise $100,000 to complete the pedestal. The statue arrives in New York Harbor in June.

·

**1886**
Pedestal is completed in April. The statue is ready and dedicated on October 28.

·

**1901**
Statue is placed under jurisdiction of the War Department.

·

**1903**
Lazarus poem is placed on tablet and affixed to pedestal.

·

**1904**
Bartholdi dies.

·

**1916**
Floodlights are installed.

·

**1924**
Statue is declared a National Monument.

**1931**
Lighting is modernized.

·

**1933**
Statue is now declared under jurisdiction of the National Park Service.

·

**1936**
50th anniversary re-dedication ceremony on October 28.

·

**1956**
Bedloe's Island is renamed Liberty Island, after Bartholdi's wishes. American Museum of Immigration is installed at base of statue.

·

**1983**
Work begins on $30-million restoration project, with money raised by donation. Restoration includes: copper skin, replacement of iron strapping with stainless steel or other material, and new stairway in statue.

·

**1986**
100th birthday celebration on July 4.

# Dimensions of the Statue

□ □ □ □ □ □

The figure itself is 151 feet tall.

The base is 65 feet tall.

The pedestal is 89 feet tall.

Including the base and the pedestal, the statue is 305 feet tall.

Liberty's mouth is 3 feet wide.

Each eye is 2 feet, 6 inches across.

Her forefinger is 8 feet long.

# Important People Who Helped in the Construction of the Statue

□ □ □ □ □ □

**Édouard René Lefebvre de Laboulaye (1811–1883):** French lawyer, teacher, and historian who gave Bartholdi the idea for the statue.

**Alexandre Gustave Eiffel (1832–1923):** French engineer who constructed the skeleton for the statue (as well as the Eiffel Tower).

**Gaget, Gauthier & Company:** The workshop of craftsmen in Paris chosen as the place to build the statue.

**Richard Morris Hunt (1827–1895):** Noted American architect who designed the pedestal for the statue.

**Charles Pomeroy Stone (1824–1887):** American engineer in charge of building the foundation on the island.

**Joseph Pulitzer (1847–1911):** Journalist and owner of the *New York World* newspaper, who helped to raise the money for the pedestal.

# Other Interesting Facts About the Statue

□ □ □ □ □ □

Liberty's crown has seven spikes which represent the seven seas and seven continents of the world.

In her raised right hand, she holds a beacon of light to welcome voyagers to America.

In her left arm, she holds a tablet inscribed in Roman numerals with the date July 4, 1776 — the date of the signing of the Declaration of Independence.

Liberty has a broken chain at her feet. Her left foot is thrust forward, to indicate progress from bondage to freedom.

# Notes on Repairs to the Statue 1980–1986

□ □ □ □ □ □

Over the hundred years since the Statue of Liberty was built, she deteriorated in a number of serious ways. Repairs and alteration never fully corrected the problems. In 1980, a group of Frenchmen began a movement to completely repair and restore the Statue of Liberty in time for her hundredth birthday in 1986. In 1982, an American committee was also formed. The French and the Americans, working together, raised money from the public in much the same way it was done over a hundred years ago. They organized a massive effort to be completed by July of 1986. The team of experts who planned the restoration was also bi-national. Money was raised in France as well as in America. The estimated cost of repairs to the statue was approximately $29 million. Money was also raised to restore Ellis Island and to establish a fund for future repairs.

# Items of Major Restoration Work

□ □ □ □ □ □
. . .

The shoulder joint in right arm was
replaced, since it had been altered
and was structurally weak.

.

The torch was removed and rebuilt.
The torch was the weakest part of the
statue. It was restored to its original
shape, since it had been modified
over the years. A new flame was
constructed.

.

Internal structural supports were
replaced.

.

New viewing platforms were installed
at the mezzanine level at the top of
the pedestal. This permits much
more of a view of the internal
structural system of the statue.

The inside skin was cleaned and
restored to its copper color. Outside,
the skin was only gently cleaned to
allow it to retain its greenish cast.
Copper, when new, is a brown
metallic color. When it is exposed to
air, it oxidizes and, if it is not
polished, will turn green.

.

The viewing platform at the crown
was rebuilt.

.

A new, all-glass elevator was
installed in the pedestal. The
hydraulic elevator was the largest
in America.

.

All the stairways were rebuilt and
improved. A new ventilation system
was installed.

**Emma Lazarus** was an American poet who, in 1883, wrote a poem called "The New Colossus" about the Statue of Liberty. This helped raise money for the Pedestal Fund. The closing lines of this poem were placed on the tablet on the pedestal in 1903.

Not like the brazen giant of Greek fame,

With conquering limbs astride from land to land;

Here at our sea–washed, sunset gates shall stand

A mighty woman with a torch, whose flame

Is the imprisoned lightning, and her name

Mother of Exiles. From her beacon–hand

Glows world–wide welcome; her mild eyes command

The air–bridged harbor that twin cities frame.

"Keep ancient lands, your storied pomp!" cries she

With silent lips. **"Give me your tired, your poor,**

**Your huddled masses yearning to breathe free,**

**The wretched refuse of your teeming shore.**

**Send these, the homeless, tempest–tost to me,**

**I lift my lamp beside the golden door!"**